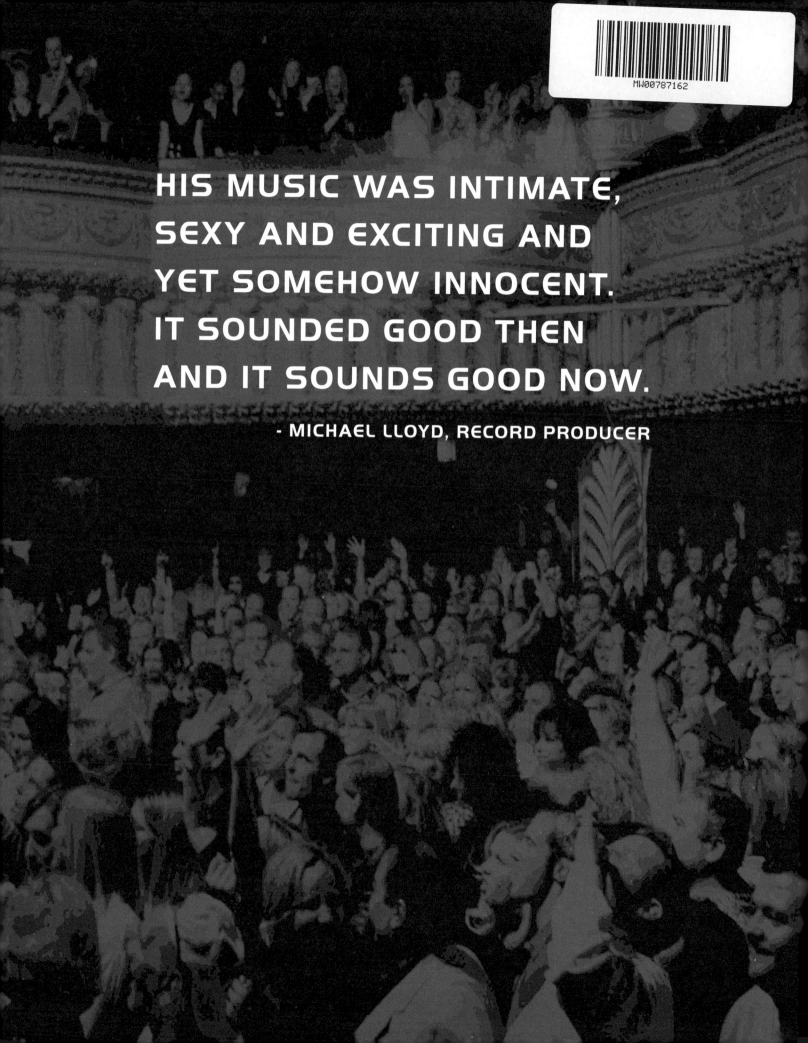

HIS MUSIC WAS INTIMATE, SEXY AND EXCITING AND YET SOMEHOW INNOCENT. IT SOUNDED GOOD THEN AND IT SOUNDS GOOD NOW.

- MICHAEL LLOYD, RECORD PRODUCER

THAT'S THE WAY I LIKE IT

THE HARRY WAYNE CASEY STORY

BY CRAIG MacINNIS

TPP TEAM POWER
PUBLISHING INC.   TRÉCARRÉ
QUEBECOR MEDIA   IM IRENE MARIE
PUBLISHING

ON JANUARY 31, 1951, AT 9:20 A.M. – A WEDNESDAY – I WAS BORN IN MIAMI, FLORIDA. GROWING UP I HARBORED DREAMS OF BECOMING A MUSICIAN, PERFORMER AND RECORDING ARTIST. IT WAS ALL I EVER THOUGHT ABOUT, OR WANTED IN LIFE. THIS BOOK IS THAT STORY IN PICTURES AND IN WORDS. I HOPE IT CONVEYS AT LEAST A SMALL SENSE OF THE FUN THAT I'VE HAD MAKING MUSIC FOR THE PAST FOUR DECADES AND COUNTING. SPECIAL THANKS TO IRENE MARIE, WHOSE INSPIRATION SET THIS PROJECT IN MOTION, AS WELL AS TO THE MANY OTHER TALENTED PEOPLE WHO DEVOTED THEIR TIME AND ENERGY TO THE PREPARATION OF THIS BOOK. THERE HAVE BEEN SO MANY PEOPLE ALONG THE WAY WHO HAVE BEEN A PART OF MY STORY – BOTH THE LIVING AND THE DECEASED – THAT I WOULD BE REMISS NOT TO INCLUDE THEM HERE. THIS BOOK IS DEDICATED TO THEM. THEY ARE:

Harry L. Casey, Jane Casey, Jim & Savina (Casey) Barnsley, Montgomery Barnsley, Casey Barnsley, Chanel Cowart, Shawn Cowart, Bill Sammeth, Mike Irvin, Mark Powers, Donald & Cass Wilson, Mel Haber, Martha Adler, the staff at Harrick Music, Wendy Melamed & Lorraine Dominguez. Allee Newhoff-Mendoza, Carlene Adams & family, Marc Serota, Lee Gatch, Sherry Smith, Steve Alaimo, Henry Stone, Clarence Reid, Betty Wright, Willie Clarke, Garry Schaeffer, Rick Finch, Jerome Smith, Robert Johnson, Beverly Champion Foster, Margaret Reynolds, Jeanette Wright, Hazel King, Debra Carter, Ronnie Smith, Denvil Liptrot, James Weaver, Charles Williams, Oliver Brown, Whit Sidner, Kenny Faulk, Vinnie Tano, all of the staff at William Morris, ICM, Pyramid for all of the wonderful years, Gayle Holcomb, Jim Ramos, Sal Michaels, Sandy Gallin, Alan David, Jim Morey, Dick Clark, Merv Griffin, Nick & Kelly Pascual & family, Jim & Beverly Ryan & family. Roger, Francis & Rhonda Swafford. Roger & Margorie Knight & family, JT & Kitty Spinks, Richard, Sandra & Donna Cantrell & families, Robert & Ruthel Cantrell & family, Terry, Elaine, Bernard, Rubilee, Tim Cantrell & family. Robert & Polly Peek & family, Abbey, Vicki, Franklin, Billy. Howard & Louise Casey, Robert Casey, Howard Casey, Fred & Betty (Casey) Dilbeck, Betsy, Brenda, Freddie, Beverly & families, Wylie Casey & family, Nina Brown & family, Katherine (Brown) Kidder & family, Alice B. (Brown) King & family, Royce Drawdy & Barbara Bell, Arthur Brown & family, Frank Brown & family. Edward Casey & family, Edith (Casey) Mitchell, Carl, Billy, Mark, Carolyn & families, Lorraine (Casey) Kortus & family, Mike & Gloria Crisante & family, Mike, Stephen, Timmy, Gloria, Freddie. Chick & Tona Shrouder, Tona, Jimmy, Armand, Deon, Jody Shrouder & families, Angel Covington, Carolyn Ballentine & family, Claudia, Robert Zulaff & Mary Ann. Armand & Marty Walterson, Savina Clark & Savina Fischer & family. Emory & Celestina, Tony, David, Tim, Bruce Griffin & families, Diane Ford, Carla Dattalo, Orlando Carrillo, Wesley Hyatt & family, Willie Simon & family, Milan Bogdan, Rick & Michelle Raymond, Barbara Stevens, Tom Boule, John Weaver, Betty Zambelli & family, Judy, Kaye, Susan & Bobby Delaney, Susan Lynn Betty Ann and the staff at Delaneys Street, Maria De Crescenzo, Ralph Herndon, Glenda Johnson, Alice Bailey, Bill Simmons, Teri De Sario, Joey Simmel & family, Bill & Sharon Pratchnick & family, Jim & Susan Reagan & family, Michael Powers & family, Charlie & Jackie Powers, Eva Davenport, Helen Baube & family, Brian Huggins & family, Sheryl Briesemiester & family, Andy Thomas, Danny Markinson, Desmond Child, Curtis Shaw, Zelda Bresland, Curtis Neely, Abundio Montez, Pat Brown, Mr. & Mrs. Duane Brown, Karen & Curtis Brown, Marion & Rod (Martin) Zamotin, Bradley, Adrian Bennett & Peggy Martin. Evelyn Mitchell, Linda & Marilee. Linda & Judy Russell, Pam Sharkis, Bill Tanner, Robert Walker & family, Charlotte Mckinnon, Kennetha Morris, Tesha Stalker, Fermin Goytisolo & Augie, Brian Scanolin, Jason Frost, Conte Bennett, Ralph Hunter, David Cabrera, Curtis Williams, Nick Marinovic, AJ Osekre, Peter Brewer, Stephen Lashley, Barry Foy, George Strakas, Chris Nathan, Thorpes Limousine NC, Carey Limousine Miami, Corporate Travel, Paula Gerson, Bruce Merrin, Roland & Victoria Phillips, George & Linda Fraser, Ron Woytowich, Tony Fick & family, Lou Pearlman, Mandy and the staff at Trans Con, Allan Crammer & family, David & Marla Bercuson, Jeanette at Frankie & Zoë's, The Lawrence's Shane, Shawn, Jay, Dwayne, Troy, Dolly & families.

To my wonderful friends at American Airlines Special Services, thank you so much. You will never know how much I appreciate your assistance. Susan Brusman & Associates & Larry Carrino, Larry & Darlene Nayman & family, Richard Pothurst, Linda, Arlene, Bill & Mrs. Tuck & families, the Holbert family, the Amerson family, the Adams family, the Falvey family, the Starkweather family, Marshall Rhodes & family, Joan Rivers & family, Scott Erickson & family, Mike Lewis, Dr Don Johnson, Junior Wade, the staff at Shula's Athletic Club, Gerhig Peterson, Doug Pinkston, Michael Booth, David Vance & Kyle, Andy & Lucille Geranis, Gus Vidal & family, the staff at Health South Miami Lakes, Craig Sculthorpe, Bob Rossi & family, Mr. & Mrs. McConnell & family, John (Footy) Kross, Allan & Sherry Jacobi, Stephen Galfas, Darcy McAllister, Mr. & Mrs. Ken Krajewski & family, Roberto Zanetti, Mrs. Rosa Wright, Mr. & Mrs. Dan Miller & family, Mr. & Mrs. Osias & family, Mr. & Mrs. Julia Wright, Mr. & Mrs. Ron Lilly, Kenny Pierce, the staff at Duke Diet & Fitness Center NC, you helped me through a difficult time, and the Team Power Publishing staff, Allan Turowetz, Craig MacInnis, Geneviève Desrosiers, Julie Desilets and Nathalie Michaud. And last but not least, to the many fans for their loyal support.

Each of you have played an important part in my career and life. May God Bless You.

With Love & Affection

TEAM POWER PUBLISHING INC.
145 West Beaver Creek Rd., Unit #1, Richmond Hill, ON L4B 1C6 CANADA

ÉDITIONS DU TRÉCARRÉ INC.
7 Chemin Bates, Outremont, QC H2V 1A6 CANADA

IRENE MARIE PUBLISHING
728 Ocean Drive, Miami Beach, FL 33139 USA

National Library of Canada Cataloguing in Publication

MacInnis, Craig
That's The Way I Like It: The Harry Wayne Casey Story / Craig MacInnis.

ISBN 2-89568-059-0

1. Casey, H. W. 2. KC & The Sunshine Band. 3. Disco musicians—United States—Biography. I. Title.

ML420.C338M15 2002   782.42164   C2002-902263-0

Legal deposit, second quarter, 2002 • National Library of Canada • Bibliothèque nationale du Québec

Official Web sites:
www.kcandthesunshineband.com
www.heykcsb.com
members.aol.com/heykcsb

Printed and bound in Canada by Quebecor World Inc. in June 2002

KEEP IT COMIN' LOVE

THE KING OF DANCE RECLAIMS HIS CROWN

Music is the mnemonic that carries us back to that giddy, life-affirming moment when we first knew that the world could be perfect. Luxuriating in the static of a tinny transistor radio at the beach, or strafed by the hot dot of a glitterball at the local discotheque, music had the power to transport us out of ourselves, to bear us aloft on a current of pure weightlessness.

Music is the communal soundtrack of our wending journey—the backdrop to first dates, prom nights, entry-level jobs, car trips to the lake, and parties under the patio lanterns at your friend's parents' split-level ranch style.

Every era has its own time signature. In the '50s it was Elvis Presley's blue-suede snarl. In the '60s it was The Beatles and their mop-top pop. Or Bob Dylan and his gruff, visionary yowl. Heard now, classic Dylan instantly evokes the heady hour of youth, the instant when we first learned there was more to life than could be gleaned from school textbooks or TV.

For those who grew up in the '70s and the moral shadow of Watergate and the Vietnam War, the song that signaled that everything would be all right again —the song that offered succor to our battered spirits, and conjures to this day a light-headed feeling in the listener—was **Get Down Tonight**.

Scorching and cataclysmic, its theme of sexual urgency triggered a national delirium and helped to write a new chapter in the Great American Songbook.

"Do a little dance, make a little love, get down tonight!" Who could resist? We immediately dropped whatever it was we'd been doing (moping about the house, mostly) and got down with KC and The Sunshine Band.

So it was that Harry Wayne Casey became synonymous with the hedonism and strut of that wonderful, chuck-it-all moment when America shed its worries and laced up its dancing shoes.

The King Of Dance had saved the day...

In the summer of 2001, KC was invited to a Salute To Disco Night at a Florida Marlins home game. The promotion was staged by the team's marketing consultant, Mike Veeck, an individual who, in the late '70s, drew the ire of dance fans everywhere with his infamous "Disco Demolition Night," in which disco records were blown up at a White Sox game at Chicago's Comiskey Park.

With KC in attendance and fans dressed in vintage disco regalia, Veeck publicly begged forgiveness: "I want to make it right," he told KC. "I want to tell you right from the bottom of my leisure suit that I'm sorry."

"I'm happy he's finally apologizing for it," said KC. "I feel redeemed. It gives closure to the whole thing."

The fact that KC never felt that The Sunshine Band's music was part of the disco fad in the first place merely added another layer of irony to the story.

"I don't think it ever was disco music, at least not the way most people think of it," KC says of his group's genre-defining "Miami Sound," which wed horns, whistles and vocal chants to a percussive, all-out-party vibe that leaned heavily, especially in the beginning, on the traditions of Bahamian "junkanoo" music, with its layered, intoxicating beats.

TOP TO BOTTOM

KC with the Florida
Marlin's mascot Billy
Song practice before
the game

RIGHT PICTURE

KC singing the National
Anthem at Pro Player Stadium
on July 12, 2001

For all the attention that would later be heaped upon global pop, a vaunted musical hybrid that found mass audiences in the late '80s and beyond, it could be argued that the magic started in south Florida when Harry Wayne Casey attended a friend's wedding. "I went to this wedding in the early '70s (for musician Clarence Reid) and they had a junkanoo band at the wedding, and the sound of that music was so infectious it was like it took over your soul," KC recalls.

"Around that same time I was also managing Timmy Thomas (another south Florida legend, famous for his 1973 hit *Why Can't We Live Together*) and we did this concert at the Capital Center in Washington, D.C., and everybody in the crowd had whistles (a short-lived fad with concert-goers of the early '70s).

"Junkanoo music already had the whistles in it—and I just thought: 'Wow!' It was just so uplifting. So that was the original idea—to have KC and The Sunshine Band be about that kind of music. Just something that got into your soul with its infectious sound."

The original name of the group, in fact, was KC And The Sunshine Junkanoo Band, which suggests that the band's original charter, beyond its affiliations with R & B, tended toward a raucous, Caribbean sensibility. "In a way it was Early Disco, if you want to call it that," says KC. "Then somebody decided, because it was played in discotheques, to call it disco music. But I don't think our music ever was disco music, I think it's always been on the edge of R & B, if anything.

KC AND MARIA PERFORMING IN NEW YORK CITY. NOVEMBER, 2001

'WOW!' IT WAS JUST SO UPLIFTING

"Because most of the time, when you dance to music, it's rhythm and blues music that you're dancing to. Not rock music. Not country music—at least not back then. Today, country music's doing the hustle and all of that stuff," he laughs. "So we not only infiltrated those other genres, we eventually infiltrated country music as well."

Most obviously, KC and The Sunshine Band foreshadowed the trend toward global pop or "world beat", which wouldn't rise to the fore until Paul Simon and David Byrne began mining Third World polyrhythms for their albums *Graceland* and *Rei Momo*, respectively, in the mid-to-late '80s. While the world was busy dancing to Simon and Byrne, few bothered to trace the lines of their musical experimentation back to their source, but it's clear in hindsight. KC—along with such hybrid-happy forerunners as Tito Puente and Harry Belafonte—stands near the front edge of an evolving sound that continues to delight millions of listeners around the world. KC didn't need any Salute To Disco Night to know that.

THAT'S THE WAY [I LIKE IT]

BY H.W. CASEY AND R. FINCH
USED BY PERMISSION FROM EMI LONGITUDE PUBLISHING

Doo doo doo doo doo doo doo
Doo doo doo doo doo doo doo

That's the way, I like it
That's the way, I like it
That's the way, I like it
That's the way, I like it

When you take me by the hand,
Tell me I'm your lovin' man
When you give me all your love and do it
Babe, the very best you can

Oh, that's the way I like it
That's the way, I like it
That's the way, I like it
That's the way, I like it

When I get to be in your arms,
When we're all all alone
When you whisper sweet in my ear,
When you turn, turn me on.

Oh, that's the way, I like it
That's the way, I like it
That's the way, I like it
That's the way, I like it

Say O.K. that's the way, that's the way
Say O.K. that's the way, that's the way
That's the way, I like it
That's the way, I like it

Doo doo doo doo doo doo doo doo doo
Doo doo doo doo doo doo doo doo doo

That's the way I like it
That's the way I like it
That's the way I like it
Say O.K. That's the way, that's the way
Say O.K. That's the way, that's the way

FROM LEFT TO RIGHT

FIRST ROW
Denvil Liptrot
James Weaver
Harry Wayne Casey

SECOND ROW
Robert Johnson
Fermin Goytisolo
Ronnie Smith

THIRD ROW
Jerome Smith
Charles Williams
Rick Finch

● ● ● ● ●

It is the first Sunday of February 2002, and Harry Wayne Casey is relaxing poolside at his rambling, ranch-style home, set at the bottom of a cul de sac in a leafy, palm-tree-lined enclave of residential Miami. Beyond the sheltering scrim of shrubs and flowers that mark his backyard property line, kids on jet-skis carve the azure surface of Biscayne Canal, sending in their wake cascades of water and noise that momentarily shatter the sun-dappled calm.

Above, red squirrels frolic in the trees while kingfishers and bluejays take turns hurling abuse at each other. It is a quietly spectacular property, blending into the verdant flora that surrounds it, secluded without being remote. Located only 25 minutes from Miami's hectic urban center, it is the place where KC has lived for nearly 30 years, through the dizzying heights of his disco-era celebrity, through the downtimes of sadness and withdrawal in the '80s and early '90s.

As a matter of coincidence, Super Bowl XXXVI will be played in a few short hours, and the eventual result of that nail-biting contest – a last-second, 20-17 upset win for the underdog New England Patriots over the heavily favored St. Louis Rams – seems hand-in-glove with the spirit of the man who is here, sipping iced tea and playing a distracted game of fetch with his tail-wagging golden retrievers, Boston and Candy.

A few days earlier, on January 31, 2002, KC celebrated his 51st birthday, and he seems happy and reflective as he gazes toward a future that's chock-a-block with recording commitments, concerts, and movie soundtrack credits (including Sunshine Band music interpreted by Destiny's Child Beyonce Knowles for the new Mike Myers sleuth-spoof, *Austin Powers 3*).

HAVING A STAR ON THE WALK OF FAME KIND OF SAYS, 'YOU'RE THERE.'
IT'S ANOTHER ONE OF THOSE

KC & The Sunshine Band WAY
W 4 AV
SERVICE ROAD

YOU'RE THERE' KIND OF MOMENTS

In August 2002, there is also the little matter of his induction into the Hollywood Walk Of Fame, a commemoration which marks KC's 30th year in the business. "I think it just substantiates the career," he says. "It legitimizes everything I did. You know, all the stuff that the critics put me down for. Having a star on the Walk Of Fame kind of says, 'You're there.' It's another one of those 'you're there' kind of moments."

In life, they say that living well is the best revenge. If that is so, then KC has outlasted his critics and shown his few remaining doubters that the music he pioneered in the '70s has fresh relevance for the new millennium. The evidence is everywhere. KC, the creator of such Zeitgeist hits as **Get Down Tonight**, **That's The Way (I Like It)**, **(Shake, Shake, Shake) Shake Your Booty**, **Keep It Comin' Love**, **Boogie Shoes** and **Please Don't Go**, has, to quote writer Jim Ruth in Pennsylvania's *Lancaster Sunday News*, "re-entered the mainstream in the slip-stream of pop music's passion for what is now called 'dance music.'"

KC's music has become a kind of cultural shorthand, earning mentions on *Friends*, *ER*, *The Simpsons*, *Saturday Night Live*, *Chicago Hope*, even David Letterman's opening monologues. Where any popular groundswell is felt, commercial interests are never far behind. The Sunshine Band's hits can be heard in commercials for General Motors, Burger King, Amoco and Denny's. The songs have also appeared in movies, including *Forrest Gump*, *Boogie Nights*, *Space Jam* and *The Nutty Professor*.

PEOPLE JUST DUG HIS VIBE. IT WAS FOR REAL

Meanwhile, hip-hop samplers have plundered the KC catalogue to infectious effect, from Jesse Jaymes' *Shake It (Like A White Girl)* to Bamboogie's roustabout classic, *Bamboogie*, which lifted the final stanzas of **Get Down Tonight**.

For Miami club deejay Ian Innocent, KC's music survives for an obvious reason — its fervent pan-cultural stylings and irresistible energy. "As far as playing his music, no matter how old the crowd is — from age 20 to 60 — you play KC's songs from back in the day and it gets a reaction that's pretty much guaranteed," says Innocent. "It's classic, timeless stuff."

Innocent, a 43-year-old London native, recalls seeing KC during the band's mid-'70s heyday at Madison Square Garden in New York, where they appeared on a triple bill with The Isley Brothers and The Jimmy Castor Bunch. "They used to have that thing where (everyone in the group) did the steps together. I can remember people saying he was just so funky for a white boy," says Innocent, who is black. "The audience he was playing to at that time was, like, 90 per cent black, but that didn't really seem to matter. People just dug his vibe. It was for real."

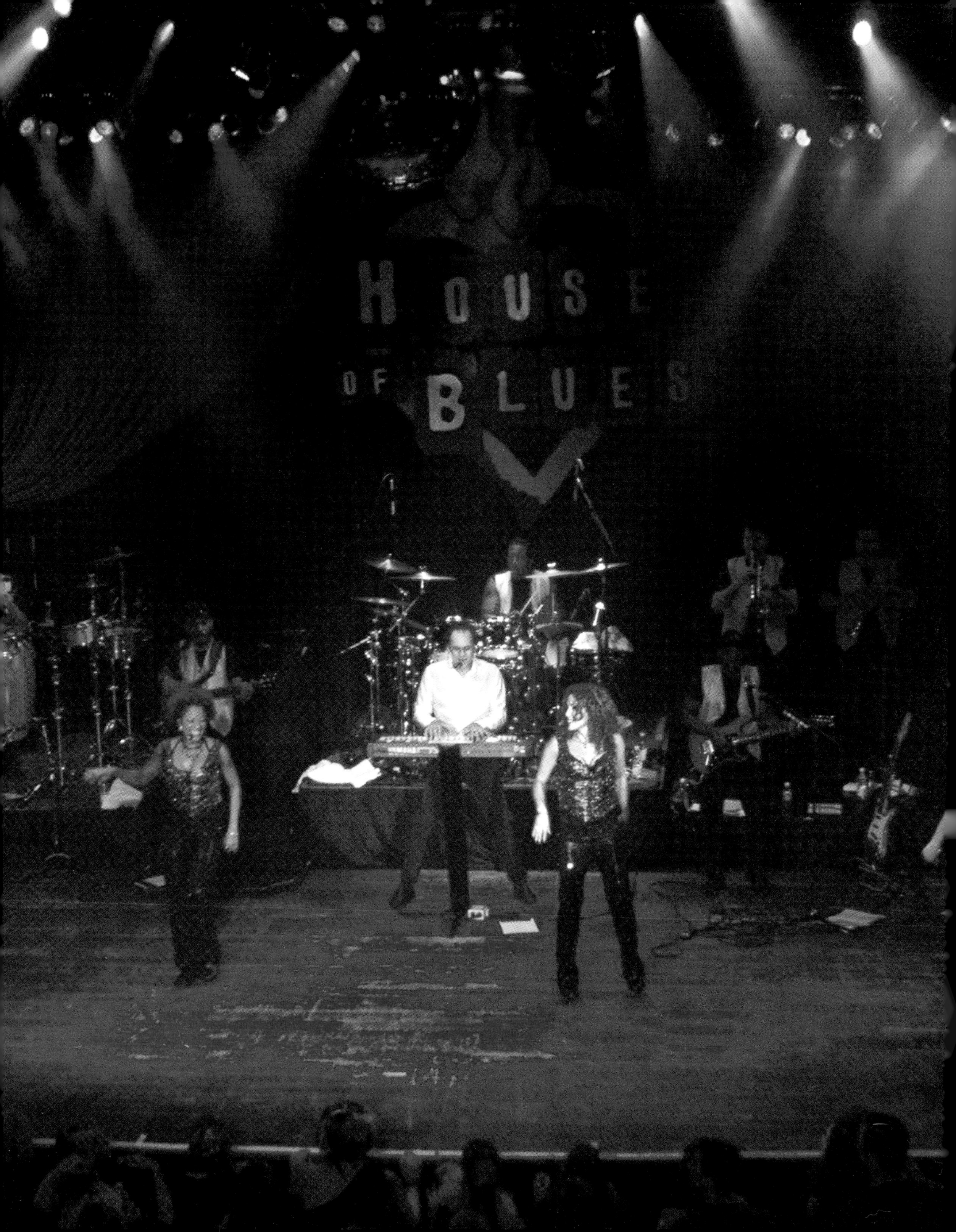
HOUSE
OF BLUES

K.C.'s friend and fellow Floridian, Desmond Child – one of the most successful songwriter/producers in the world, whose credits include Ricky Martin's "Livin' La Vida Loca" as well as major hits for KISS, Cher, Bon Jovi and Aerosmith – notes that KC was the purveyor of a regional sound that conquered the world and put Florida on the map.

"KC had a tropical air to his music, which was natural to happen because we're the gateway to the Caribbean," says Child. "That's why the music that came out of Miami had a fusion of R&B and gospel and tropical flavors.

"He created his own sound," adds Child, who met KC two years ago when the latter was being honored by the Florida chapter of the National Academy Of Recording Arts and Sciences [NARAS]. Child sits on the NARAS board of governors. They've been fast friends ever since.

"Usually people become buddy-buddy when they want something out of each other," says Child, who runs his own record label, Deston Entertainment. "He's not that way. He's really a pure spirit. KC has a great sense of humor. He's warm. He's sincere. He's very caring."

For a time in the early '70s, Desmond's mother was the receptionist at T.K. Records, where all the early Sunshine Band records were made. "She would bring home records and that's how I became aware of him as a kid," says Child. "I was going out to dance clubs and hanging out and listening to the music. I think everybody was really proud that KC was one of us, from Florida and all that."

TOP TO BOTTOM

Desmond Child
Desmond Child & KC
at the 2001 Recording
Academy Florida Herves
Awards In June 2001

Child says that his hit song, *I Was Made For Loving You*, which he wrote for the rock band KISS, "was definitely influenced by the dance music of that time, which was KC."

Adds Child: "He was the architect of a new sound, which was anthemic and had elements of rock and pop mixed in with R&B. He's had an amazing influence in the way people perceive dance music and pop music."

Punning on the name of another famous south Florida pop export, Child laughs: "He was making the 'Sound' before Miami had a 'Machine.'"

Bernie Lopez, the publisher and owner of discomusic.com, widely regarded as the Internet's best and most comprehensive disco website, argues that racial factors shouldn't be ignored when assessing the impact KC and The Sunshine Band had on the world.

"I have a feeling," says Lopez, a New Jersey native, "that a lot of it had to do with race.

THE ONE COMMONALITY WITH ALL OF THE SONGS BY KC AND RICK FINCH,

WAS THE UPBEAT MESSAGE,

"And by that I mean that at the time when I was growing up most of the kids would turn on TV and they would watch *American Bandstand* on Saturday morning. But there was a select minority that didn't want to watch that because they thought it was uncool. They would watch *Soul Train*, which was the black program. To be perfectly honest, there was a lot more prejudice going on back then because I remember when I was growing up in the '70s the word 'n....' would be used freely all the time, and there was a certain stigma attached to listening to black music.

PERFORMING IN CHICAGO, MAY 2002

THE SUGGESTION THAT YOU COULD HAVE FUN

"This is where KC and The Sunshine Band ties in, because here you have a group that has a funky sound and if you really weren't paying attention you'd think they were an all-black group, but they weren't. Their two frontmen (KC and former songwriting partner and bassist Rick Finch) were white, and I think that kind of gave everybody the OK."

Lopez's theory that KC and The Sunshine Band were cross-racial pioneers, riding their multi-cultural funk caravan up the charts and raising America's consciousness in the process, is a theory seconded by Beverly Foster, the longtime Sunshine Band backing singer. "The one commonality with all of the songs by KC and Rick Finch, to me, was the upbeat message, the suggestion that you could have fun," says Foster.

"People were ready to embrace positive things. We had just come through the Vietnam War. We had friends that we lost in the war. And we were all old enough to remember JFK and Robert Kennedy and Martin Luther King and all the civil unrest in the country."

Foster, who stopped touring a couple of years ago to recuperate from breast cancer, feels that the Sunshine Band was at the forefront of liberal, inclusionary thinking when it came to its lineup. "You had the two white guys, KC and Rick, then there was Fermin, the percussionist, who was Cuban, and nine blacks. And then also there was that gender mix with the male-female combination."

KC says the group's cross-cultural sound was deliberate: "That was part of the whole thing, to break the racial barriers. I'm white, but I was told that I sounded too 'black' and that I'd never make it. So that was another objective, to break down the racial barriers. When you tell me I can't do something I'm going to show you that I can do it. I went to audition for a local band one time and they said I had too much 'soul.' They were the top group in Miami at the time," he adds, declining to mention them by name. ("I don't want to rub it in any more than I have to.")

"The crazy thing is they would play stuff like The Temptations and things like that," KC recalls, "and here they are telling me I have too much soul?" As a teenager in the '60s, KC was profoundly influenced by Motown and its various soul-rock offshoots, which would form the creative bedrock for his own musical ideas a decade later. "I always loved Motown. I grew up not only with Motown, but there was Joe Cocker and that whole thing going on. There was Blood, Sweat & Tears and Chicago, The Rascals. All those things became my influence. I loved that whole type of sound, from Otis Redding to Aretha Franklin."

SOUND YOUR FUNKY HORN

BUILDING A DANCEFLOOR DYNASTY

The Jesuits have a saying—"Give me the boy till he is seven and I will show you the man."

The Jesuits never got Harry Wayne Casey. He was raised a Pentecostal, which still gave him plenty to rebel against. By age seven he was already showing early signs of the booty-shaking, tub-thumping, ball-of-hormonal energy he would become as frontman for the world's most hyperkinetic, quasi-disco orchestra, 20 years later.

"He was very active and energetic," said mother Jane Casey. "He entertained all the other kids all the time."

They say location is opportunity, and for KC, the venue of his first great "performance" was Hialeah, the Miami suburb where his parents moved when he was a tot.

"I'm very lucky," KC says. "I grew up in a neighborhood with a lot of kids. All the families were very close. I had parades down the street, and would put on little shows. We'd take sheets to make curtains and the whole thing, so I was kind of the entertainment director of the block.

"At times, I think one of the running jokes was: What was I going to build in my backyard? I had a treehouse upstairs with a store on the bottom, and I'd build rides, rollercoasters, everything."

If there was an incidental soundtrack to young Harry's backyard productions, it was supplied by his music-loving mom, who flooded their house with the latest from Ray Charles, The Flamingoes, Nat King Cole.

She nicknamed her only son "Sparky," after a character from the 1944 movie, *Home In Indiana*, starring Walter Brennan and Lon McCallister. KC's mom *loved* the movies, in marked contrast to KC's grandmother, a loving matriarch who put religion first. "She was strict but we loved each other very much," KC says of his grandmother.

KC AND HIS MOM JANE. MIAMI BEACH, FLORIDA

Like most kids, KC took piano lessons, that hoary rite of passage that is meant to instill – note-by-note, scale-by-scale – an appreciation for conformity and melody. "It wasn't until my younger sister Savina showed interest in wanting to play that we actually got a piano at the house," he recalls. "It was because of her wanting to take lessons that I ended up taking them too."

Alas, KC didn't last long as a young Rachmaninoff-in-training: "I've always wanted my own identity," he says, explaining his aversion to sheet music. "I've always had my own rhythm, and I think maybe it was hard to latch on to 'one, two, three, four'."

During that time KC borrowed five hundred dollars from his dear friends Don and Cass Wilson to make his first record. "Don and Cass really believed in me" KC reminisces. KC sold his first record at a Recordsville store in the Palm Springs Mall where he had gotten a job. He sold a few copies, but it wasn't a big hit. After graduating from Hialeah High School, he started college at Miami-Dade North, taking a medley of courses including business administration, psychology and music theory.

It was a hectic schedule, and he was making decent money as a record store clerk. One day, however, he announced he was leaving the world of retail for a new job – one that didn't actually pay anything.

TOP TO BOTTOM

LEFT PAGE
June 61 – With his sister Savina
"Sparky"
Performing in Miami

RIGHT PAGE
KC's first band, Russ Hammerstraum,
KC and Bill Tuck

IF YOU LOVE FOOTBALL AND CAN'T BE THE QUARTERBACK,
BE THE GUY WHO BRINGS THE WATER

KC had started hanging out at the new T.K. studios—a combination record warehouse and attic recording facility owned by R & B music legend Henry Stone. It was here, in the fullness of time, that he would rendezvous with his destiny—and his new musical collaborator, Rick Finch.

"My biggest break was finding this little record company, this little recording studio," he recalls. "I mean, there was Criteria in Miami, but you had to have money to get into Criteria to record a record.

"T.K. was not like Criteria. Criteria was a recording studio where everybody from the Who's Who list paid big money to record there. T.K. was this private thing. They were making their own records and distributing them."

Steve Alaimo, T.K. Productions' vice president and head of A&R, years ago reflected on the origins of the south Florida recording industry in a newspaper interview. "Around 1970, Henry Stone and I decided we were going to start a record company in Florida," Alaimo said. "And we just worked real hard and it worked. For one thing, the weather's so good down here. L.A., New York... it's more comfortable here. We built a little studio. We just added on and got bigger."

AT LEAST YOU'RE DOING WHAT YOU LOVE

In an article on the area's burgeoning recording scene, *The Miami Herald* nailed T.K.'s downmarket vibe: "T.K. Productions is wedged into a dead-end street behind the Winn-Dixie warehouses and just off the flight path of nearby Miami International Airport. The place is the perfect illustration of the term ramshackle."

IN T.K. STUDIO. THE EARLY YEARS.

Ramshackle or not, to the young KC the studio was a stereophonic Eden.

"My first break was being introduced to (T.K. regulars) Clarence Reid and Willie Clark," he recalls. "Also at T.K. there was this little room off the reception area with a piano in it, so I'd go in there and I'd be writing little songs, or playing piano and singing.

"Henry Stone, I think, saw that I had some talent. I proved to them that I was ambitious enough to do anything and not ask for anything in return."

His early days at T.K. were testament to his youthful vigor, as he practically redefined the term "gofer" in a bid to ingratiate himself to his new bosses.

"Well, that's how you grow," he shrugs. "I guess there wasn't an intern (at T.K.), but I made myself the intern. It took five years, five years to get to where I really wanted to be.

AT THE OFFICES – **FROM THE LEFT** RECORDING ARTIST BETTY WRIGHT, H. W. CASEY [KC] T.K.'S ITALIAN REP, PRODUCER/WRITER WILLIE CLARKE, T.K. PRESIDENT HENRY STONE, RICK FINCH, T.K. RECORDING ARTIST BENNY LATIMORE.

"I say this a lot of times: Do what you love in life. Head for that direction and work in that area. If you love football and can't be the quarterback, be the guy who brings the water! At least you're doing what you love.

"If you can't be a model, get behind a desk and answer the phones, be an agent, be the one that dresses the model, does the makeup, the hair, but be happy about it. Don't be miserable because you're not them."

So it was that KC proved his mettle at T.K., doing odd jobs which included processing returns, boxing up records, answering the phones, sweeping the floor and, eventually, playing keyboards in recording sessions.

Rick Finch, meanwhile, was doing much the same, trying to learn the business from the bottom up as a trainee technician and bass player.

"I was mesmerized by the making of records and how the whole thing worked – anything that made the speaker go 'boom' and made the cone go in and out," Finch once told a writer. "I made it my business to be a pain in the ass down there."

Like KC, Finch was granted access to a world he could previously only dream about. "I didn't know much about the business. When you're young, it's a magic thing, you know?"

He added: "Clarence Reid would be doing pilot vocals for Betty Wright, and there would be other things going on, like these X-rated Blowfly records. That was some of the first stuff that I produced and engineered – as a guest! Within a year, I could run the console and do productions.

"Willie Clarke was the first one to let me assist on anything. 'Last Tango In Paris' by Antique was my first production by myself. I was 14 or 15. Steve Alaimo was also someone I was a pain in the ass to, because I asked too many questions."

KC & The Su

Critics have always been intrigued by the alchemy of great artistic collaborations. Lennon and McCartney are felt to have clicked because their personalities —Lennon's acerbic wit, McCartney's sweeter world view—furnished the animating tension that gave The Beatles' lyrical relevance and chart power.

The chemistry between KC and Rick is trickier. Even Steve Alaimo admitted he never quite managed to break down the duo's respective roles in the studio: "In the beginning, I had my doubts about which one was doing it," Alaimo told a reporter. "I'm not sure to this day which one. I just know that together they did it. Finch did it all, then KC did it all. If anyone out there knows the answer, they're lying."

For his part, KC says of his partnership with Finch: "We were good friends and our talents worked very well together. They complemented each other. We were really a good team."

As Brian Chin has noted in his condensed history of the group for Rhino Records: "Not only were the boys thrifty, but, thanks to the sessions they had already played in the studio (as backing musicians), they were also fast."

Chin notes that the rhythm track for *Rock Your Baby*, the Casey/Finch duo's breakthrough production hit in 1974, was done in just 45 minutes, with only one additional player, Jerome Smith, on guitar.

The lilting ballad arrangement didn't really fit KC's singing style, so it was eventually offered to George McCrae, who knocked it off in two takes and had a crossover No. 1 R & B/pop hit in the summer of 1974. *Rock Your Baby* set the table for the coming disco craze and sold a reported 11 million copies in the process.

Buoyed by their success, KC and Rick stepped up their work for other T.K. stablemates, co-writing Betty Wright's Grammy-winning hit, *Where Is The Love*, and producing Gwen McCrae's *Move Me Baby* and Jimmy "Bo" Horne's *Gimme Some* (Part One).

Even before that, the Casey/Finch magic had been caught on a couple of their own embryonic singles: **Blow Your Whistle** in '73 and **Sound Your Funky Horn**, from early '74, which served notice of bigger and better things to come.

SOUND YOUR FUNKY HORN

BY H.W. CASEY AND C. REID
USED BY PERMISSION FROM EMI LONGTITUDE PUBLISHING

Baseman burn the bottom
Drummer, drum the beat
Tenorman come take your stand
Everybody on your feet

Everybody, sound your funky horn
Come on, get down
Everybody, sound your funky horn
Come on, get down

Guitar keep the rythm
Congas add the groove
When the main man gets on his horn
Everybody's got to move

Everybody, sound your funky horn
Come on, get down
Everybody, sound your funky horn
Come on, get down

Everybody, sound your funky horn
Come on, get down
Everybody, sound your funky horn
Come on, get down

Baseman Mr. Drummer
Keep a smile on your face
Guitar, Mr. Conga
Keep on, keepin' a steady pace

Everybody, sound your funky horn
Come on, get down
Everybody, sound your funky horn
Come on, get down

Everybody, come on
Let me hear it, let me hear it

FORTY-EIGHT CITIES IN 24 DAYS: THAT'S JUST THE WAY IT WAS.

IT WAS ABSOLUTELY CRAZY, DRIVING

FIRST BAND PHOTO IN 1973, JEROME SMITH, RICK FINCH, ROBERT JOHNSON, KC

"When we did **Blow Your Whistle** (which reached No. 17 on the R & B chart in 1973), the sound didn't translate onto the tape the way we had heard it in person," KC says, shaking his head as if it still stumps him.

"I don't know why. Some of the feel was there, but it just wasn't what I had heard in my head. So by the time the next record came out (**Sound Your Funky Horn**, which rose to No. 21 on the R & B chart), it was going to be a little different because it just wasn't coming across the way I had envisioned it. I always loved horns and I added that onto the new record."

By the time of **Do It Good**, the group's first full-length album, released in 1974, The Sunshine Band's music boasted a surging, bum-wagging swagger that seemed entirely its own thing yet subtly aligned with other traditions, from Motown to funk.

Call it good timing, or fate, but the infectious tunes KC and company were churning out in Florida meshed perfectly with the British "northern soul" explosion then rocking clubs in Great Britain. The band's third single, **Queen Of Clubs**, which had been slow to find altitude in the U.S., shot straight into England's Top 10.

To bolster their overseas popularity, the group was sent out on a gruelling month-long tour of Britain. For KC, the trip was made worse by a sudden illness the day before their trans-Atlantic flight.

FROM ONE PLACE TO ANOTHER IN A FOG

"I just wasn't feeling well that whole day. I was green. I just thought it was the 'flu' but what I had was acute appendicitis.

"I was very upset because I felt like I was letting everyone down. We had prepared for this tour and now I was letting the side down."

Adhering to that old bromide The Show Must Go On (which must have been coined by a tour manager rather than the performers who have to do the actual work), KC had an emergency appendectomy and managed to keep his commitment to his bandmates—and his new British fans.

"Forty-eight cities in 24 days," he says, recalling the whiplash pace. "That's just the way it was. It was absolutely crazy, driving from one place to another in a fog.

"It would be the middle of the night, driving at incredible speeds to get to the next show, which could be two hours away, then getting up the next morning and doing it all over again."

Afterwards, KC told *The Miami News* that the pre-tour surgery had affected his ability to perform to his usual kinetic standards: "I mean, here we are doing two shows a night and the English press is right there by our side slamming us for not being visual enough. Just unbelievable. I don't think they understand it's pretty hard to jump around when your stomach's just been split up the middle."

Seeing for the first time how crowds had reacted to their music, KC and the band returned from the English jaunt "really energized," he says. "We went in to the studio and that's when we recorded **Get Down Tonight** and **That's The Way (I Like It)**."

Much has been written about **Get Down Tonight**, which became the band's first No. 1 hit in the summer of 1975, setting in motion a prolific cycle that would eventually see the group chart four No. 1 pop singles in a year, tying a record set by The Beatles.

Even more than a quarter century after the world first boogied to **Get Down Tonight**, its opening theme, and its lunging, giddy tempo, presents an irresistible goad to the casual listener. Silly and sensual, fun-loving and seductive, it stands as one of the greatest party anthems of all time.

As Greg Baker wrote in a retrospective on KC's music for Miami's *New Times*: "KC And The Sunshine Band were significant innovators, and their music still sends shock waves after all these years. He and his cohorts invented what would come to be known as the Miami Sound, and they took it to its apex.

"No one since has been able to touch their melding of R&B's soulfulness and dance music's primal beat. KC's music endures because 10 or 15 years ago it was about 20 years ahead of its time."

KC'S MUSIC ENDURES BECAUSE 10 OR 15 YEARS AGO IT WAS ABOUT

20 YEARS AHEAD OF ITS TIME

[SHAKE, SHAKE, SHAKE]

SHAKE YOUR BOOTY

BY H.W. CASEY AND R. FINCH
USED BY PERMISSION FROM EMI LONGTITUDE PUBLISHING AND HARRICK MUSIC

Aw, ev'rybody get on the floor, let's dance
Don't fight the feelin'
Give yourself a chance

Shake, shake, shake, shake, shake, shake
Shake your booty. Shake your booty
Shake, shake, shake, shake, shake, shake
Shake your booty. Shake your booty

Aw, you can, you can do it very well
You're the best in the world, I can tell
Shake, shake, shake, shake, shake, shake
Shake your booty. Shake your booty
Shake, shake, shake, shake, shake, shake
Shake your booty. Shake your booty

Aw, shake, shake, shake, shake
Shake, shake, shake, shake
Aw, shake, shake, shake
Shake, shake, shake, shake your booty
Shake your booty. Shake, shake, shake
Shake, shake, shake, shake your booty
Aw, shake, shake, shake, shake
Shake your booty

Aw, don't fight the feeling
Shake, shake, shake, shake
Shake your booty
Aw, give yourself a chance
Shake, shake, shake, shake
Shake your booty

You can do it, do it
Shake, shake, shake, shake
Shake your booty
Come on mama. Shake, shake, shake
Shake your booty

Woo, woo, woo, woo, woo, woo, woo
Woo, woo, woo, shake, shake, shake, shake
Shake your booty. Aw, drop down, sister
Shake, shake, come on
Shake, come on your booty
Aw, your booty. Shake, shake, come on

GET DOWN TONIGHT

KC DEFINES A GENERATION

BY THE TIME THEY ARRIVED HOME,

GET DOWN TONIGHT WAS NO. 1,

During their second European tour in the summer of 1975, the band suddenly took off in America. By the time they arrived home, **Get Down Tonight** was No. 1, and everything had changed forever.

"The only thing that came close to what I witnessed with our group was a phenomenon like The Beatles," KC remembered for VH1's *Behind The Music.* "It was just that kind of pandemonium, that kind of craziness."

"It just broke wide open," added Rick Finch. "When we came back to Miami, off the airplane, we were like instant stars."

To celebrate their freshly-minted celebrity, the band put on an outdoor show only 23 hours after arriving back from Europe. They were greeted by 3,500 hometown fans at Miami's Virginia Beach, where the stage set-up was primitive, to say the least. The band played right on the ground.

As music critic Jon Marlowe deadpanned in his review for *The Miami News*: "The promoters seemed to have spared every expense on this outdoor concert, including a stage."

Still, it was a joyous occasion. George McCrae, riding the fame of *Rock Your Baby*, his hit from the previous year, showed up to lend a hand on vocals, blending with the "pretty young ladies" of KC's backing group, Fire—Beverly Foster, Jeannette Wright and Margaret Reynolds.

AND EVERYTHING HAD CHANGED FOREVER

As Marlowe reported: "The crowd passes a rousing version of **Queen Of Clubs** by in their constant demands for **Get Down Tonight**. When KC and The Sunshine Band finally give it to them, the place erupts. People jump into the water separating the band and the audience, everybody is up dancing and clapping, and as the group slides into the final notes of their disco anthem, they are totally enveloped by their hometown fans."

"All I want to do is create happy music," KC told Marlowe. "That's what this whole band is about."

The instantly accelerated pace of life and the surging, mob-like crowds wherever they toured in the mid '70s, left KC – and still leaves KC, even a quarter century later – dazed and dumbfounded. "Don't ask me to tell stories from the road. I don't remember the stories," he pleads with a grin.

The blur of finding oneself as the center of attention in the world's hottest band, was not a simple thing to endure, no matter how great it felt "for those two hours each night when you're up there, singing and dancing and connecting with the fans."

Percussionist Fermin Goytisolo, the only Sunshine Band member from the original group who performs with KC to this day, recalls the panic of finding oneself, literally overnight, playing to crowds 100 times larger than anything previously experienced.

"I never thought **Get Down Tonight** was going to be so big," says Goytisolo. "I mean, I never did. And KC called me and said, 'You want to go out on the road?' I was really scared at first. All those crowds. I used to get butterflies in my stomach."

It turned out that Goytisolo's trepidation was justified.

"I think it was San Francisco," Goytisolo recalls. "We were coming out of the stadium when all of a sudden we're coming through this hallway and this fan grabs KC's jacket and picks him up in the air and is holding him up and choking him, you know?

"And we're all trying to pull him down, and he's going: 'Don't pull me down, you're choking me!'"

TOP TO BOTTOM

Mike Douglas Show, 1975 [1 & 2]

Percussionist Fermin Goytisolo

Beverly Foster remembers how the audiences, in those early days, often didn't know what to expect when they showed up for a concert.

"One of the things that stands out in my mind, was that when KC came out, there was like this *chant* in the audience: 'He's white!' I mean, nobody knew. His music was very soulful, and so I think it was a contradiction to a lot of people. The music had a real R&B edge to it, so everybody assumed that KC was black."

It wouldn't take long for the crowds to get with the program, because the hits had only just begun. After **Get Down Tonight** ascended the charts, so did **That's The Way (I Like It)** and **(Shake, Shake, Shake) Shake Your Booty**.

In 1977 the band returned with **I'm Your Boogie Man**, another No. 1 hit, and **Keep It Comin' Love**, which went to No. 1 on the R&B charts, and No. 2 on the pop charts.

All the while, Finch and KC continued to gather credits for their work on other people's projects. The Cinderella tandem picked up a Grammy for their writing contribution to Betty Wright's *Where Is The Love*, and in 1978, KC notched two more Grammys as a performer and producer on the album of the year, *Saturday Night Fever*.

While KC was enjoying the adulation, he was also feeling something else which he couldn't quite put his finger on. Anomie, maybe. Or a vague feeling of being pushed past his limit, of being entrapped by his celebrity, of feeling "panicked."

"There's the thing of being afraid of it," he says, choosing his words carefully. "Being afraid of what comes with that whole lifestyle."

KC WAS BLACK

LEFT TO RIGHT: SAXOPHONISTS DENVILL LATROT AND EUGENE TIMMONS

KC says loneliness was his constant companion on the road, despite the paradox of being surrounded by so many people. "I remember a show in Pittsburgh, Pennsylvania, and looking out a window and seeing the crowd down there and wishing I could be down there with them, knowing I couldn't. That made me very lonely, and very detached and isolated. That wasn't fun."

GET DOWN TONIGHT

BY R.W. CASEY AND R. FINCH
USED BY PERMISSION FROM EMI LONGITUDE PUBLISHING

Baby, babe let's get together
Honey, honey me and you
And do the things, oh, do the things
That we like to do

Oh, do a little dance, make a little love
Get down tonight, get down tonight,
Do a little dance, make a little love
Get down tonight, get down tonight

Baby, babe it's meet you same place
Same time, where we can, oh, get together
And ease up our mind

Oh, do a little dance, make a little love
Get down tonight, get down tonight
Do a little dance, make a little love
Get down tonight, get down tonight, baby

Do a little dance, make a little love
Get down tonight, get down tonight
Do a little dance, make a little love
Get down tonight, get down tonight

Get down, get down, get down, get down
Get down tonight baby

We wo wo wo wo wo wo wo

Get down, get down, get down, get down
Get down tonight

Na na na na na na na na na na na

FROM LEFT TO RIGHT

- Dick Clark
- Mac Davis
- Captain & Tenille
- Marie Osmond
- Michael Jackson
- Ron Wood of the Rolling Stones

KC performing with Donna Summer on the Mac Davis Show

FROM LEFT TO RIGHT

● Donna Summer and KC

● Whitney Houston

● Stevie Wonder

● Dinah Shore Show

● KC, Mike Douglas, Milton Berle and Jackie Gleason

● With Don Rickles and Merv Griffin on the Merv Griffin Show

Then there were the critics, many of whom considered disco a barely-tolerable musical genre—when they considered it at all.

Peter Goddard, *The Toronto Star's* veteran rock critic, in the summer of '77, covered one of the most famous Sunshine Band concerts ever, at an outdoor, government-run pavilion called Ontario Place Forum. Built along a spit reaching out from the shores of Lake Ontario near downtown Toronto, the Forum was located just across the way from Exhibition Place, which was then the home of major league baseball's Toronto Blue Jays.

"Add those 30,000 screaming disco-rock fans to a Blue Jay game across the road and it equalled chaos," wrote a reporter for the *Toronto Sun*, under the banner headline: "SHAKE YOUR BOOTY!"

"Ontario Place officials closed the gates to incoming traffic, both auto and people, at 6:30 p.m. Concert time was 8:30. Some of the fans locked outside broke through the gates and climbed fences only to be hustled off by waiting (police) officers. Some fans tore bleacher seats situated along the lakeshore for boating exhibitions and floated their way into Ontario Place a few hundred feet away."

"I remember that concert," KC laughs. "People were trying to swim over to see us."

That was the news story, but Peter Goddard's review of the concert put the event in an altogether different light. Goddard's review offers one of the best mid-'70s defences of a style of music that was then being unfairly pilloried by most music journalists on the continent.

"Since their first big hit, **Get Down Tonight**, two summers ago," wrote Goddard, "this Florida-based band has been all but ignored by an increasingly adult and increasingly snooty rock establishment.

"Cool disc jockeys on FM radio won't play their music; it's disco, and disco is bad for the image. Besides, KC and company attract the people the rock establishment is ignoring, deliberately or otherwise – the teenagers and those even younger."

It continued: "KC is not out to improve minds, to be hip, or to do anything a rock star is supposed to. He is just out to have a good time and make lots of money letting others have a good time."

Goddard also caught something essential about the appeal of Harry Wayne Casey as a performer. "There's a streak of madness in his eyes and he has a wicked grin. His songs, each of them equally simple, have a hint of easy-going sex hidden just beneath the lyrics."

The last word on the Ontario Place show, however, went to a beleaguered security cop: "They shouldn't have had the concert here. I guess they won't do it again, at least not for this KC group."

Beverly Foster says the strangest road incident occurred in Rio. "We were all sitting around the pool at the hotel, having a couple of drinks, and we wanted to listen to some music. It was a gorgeous night and so KC and I decided to go to his room to get his tape-player. So we get on this elevator and this elevator starts moving upward at, like, 75 miles an hour, speeding past every floor, totally out of control!

"We're pretty sure that we're going to die," she says. "We're holding each other, talking about what great friends we've been to each other: 'I love you!' 'I love you!' Then all of a sudden, after we zoom past our floor, way up near the top of the shaft, all of a sudden the elevator comes to a dead halt.

"The door opens on to white marble floors with columns. We thought we were in heaven. And there were these old people there saying: 'C'mon, c'mon, we've been waiting for you!' We were like, 'Uh, uh, no way!'"

LEFT TO RIGHT: KC WITH TERI DE SARIO, GEORGE McCRAE

They had accidentally taken the express elevator, which had deposited them at a penthouse seniors convention. The symbolism wasn't lost on Foster, or KC for that matter, who laughs when reminded.

"That was amazing. We were rocketing out of control," he says, conceding the story's ready-made metaphor.

By 1978, disco seemed to have shot its bolt. KC and the band continued plying the charts with **Boogie Shoes** and **The Same Old Song**, but neither got into the

LIKE A GOOD TIME TO STEP BACK

Top 10. However, the band came roaring back with another No. 1 in 1980, the wistful ballad, **Please Don't Go**, plus their R&B scorcher, **Do You Wanna Go Party**.

KC also had a duet with Teri De Sario on a version of the Barbara Mason soul pleaser, **Yes I'm Ready**, which went to No. 2 on the poplist as the 1970s drew to a close. But there was no denying it: the nation's disco party was over, and the band, so used to its forward momentum, so used to gathering up hits and playing to huge crowds wherever it went, was caught unawares.

"We didn't think about the end," Rick Finch told *Behind The Music*. "We just kept doing it and doing it."

It is in the nature of all bands to feed off their momentum, to generate energy from the daily act of performing in front of thousands of adoring fans. More than a few groups, including The Kinks and Lynyrd Skynyrd, have written songs about the glories of the road, which can quickly turn into a dead-end street when the fun stops.

"At a certain point, being part of a band—even a band as great as ours—just wasn't fun any more," says KC. "It just felt like a good time to step back."

DO YOU WANNA GO PARTY

BY H.W. CASEY AND R. FINCH
USED BY PERMISSION FROM EMI LONGITUDE PUBLISHING AND HARRICK MUSIC

Ooh, ah, party, ooh, ah, party
Ooh, ah, party, ooh, ah, party

Do you wanna go party
We'll get funky there, party
Drink a little wine, party
Have a funky time, party

Come on baby, sexy lady
Let's go out tonight
We'll go party
We'll go dancin'
Let's go get satisfied

Ooh, ah, party, ooh, ah, party
Ooh, ah, party, ooh, ah, party

Come on baby, sexy lady
Let yourself unwind
I wanna love you
Kiss and hug you
Make it last all night

Ooh, ah, party, ooh, ah, party
Ooh, ah, party, ooh, ah, party

Do you wanna go party
We'll get funky there, party
Drink a little wine, party
Have a funky time, party

Ooh, ah, ooh, ah
Ooh, ah, ooh, ah

Do you wanna go party
Do you wanna go party
We'll get funky there, party
Drink a little wine, party
Have a funky time, party

Party
Party
Party
[Repeat]

WHO DO YA LOVE, 1978

DO YOU WANNA GO PARTY, 1979

THEIR GREATEST HITS, 1980

DO IT GOOD, 1974

KC AND THE SUNSHINE BAND
... AND MORE, 1975

PART 3 ... AND MORE, 1976

SPACE CADET, 1981

THE PAINTER, 1981

ALL IN A NIGHT'S WORK, 1982

KC TEN, 1983

OH YEAH!, 1993

I'll BE THERE FOR YOU, 2001

PLEASE DON'T GO

RETURN TO ZERO: KC ESCAPES THE NOISE

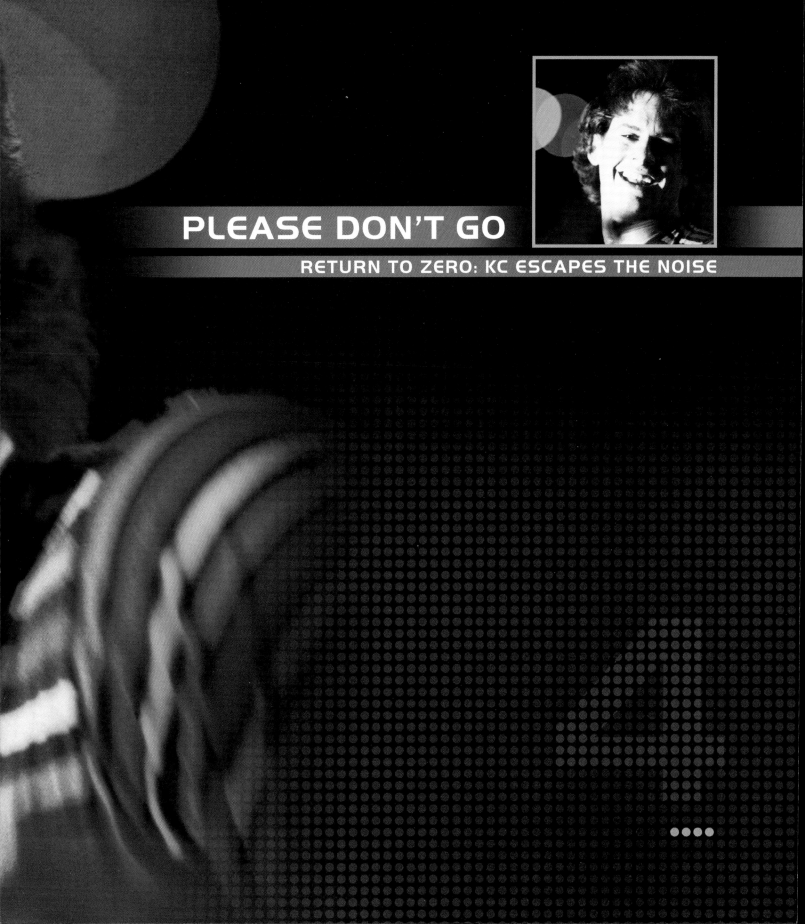

It is axiomatic that anything permitted to rise to great heights – as KC's music rose; stratospherically, in the gusts of an irresistible force – will just as surely fall back to Earth, brought low by the same mysterious things that gave it lift.

Or you could simply say what the Sunshine Band's longtime percussionist Fermin Goytisolo says: "I think it's like with every band. You get five or six good years, a hit record, and then you kind of run out of ideas."

Or: your ideas no longer seem to play to an increasingly fickle public. Or: your record company perversely refuses to release a sure-fire single. Or: your personal life takes a series of savage, unpredictable turns – a car accident, the death of a beloved parent – that drag you to the depths of despair.

For KC and The Sunshine Band, the '80s began with the group's departure from T.K. Records. KC felt that the label, his creative home for the previous decade – a place where he had gone from the early drudgery of boxing other artists' records to selling 75 million of his own – was guilty of neglecting their most profitable band – his – in favor of newer, younger acts.

KC's last record for T.K. Records, **Space Cadet**

He does not wish to make too much of this falling out with T.K. and says he bears no grudges after all this time. Prodded a little, however, he elaborates on his early-'80s mindset.

"I remember walking around (the T.K. offices) just before we had a new album coming out, and they didn't have our poster up on the wall. There was nothing that felt like they were supporting our new project," he says.

"I just felt, at that time, a little betrayed, or neglected. Life's too short to bear a grudge, but I just thought that, as a business decision, it didn't make sense to be with a label that didn't seem interested in working our records."

KC signed with the major label, Epic, and released two albums—1981's *The Painter*, followed, the next year, by *All In A Night's Work*, neither of which exactly burned up the charts in the era of New Wave, a British-American hybrid that had replaced disco in all the fashionable clubs—and on the charts.

With its penchant for aloof stagecraft, sardonic lyrics and ironic retro fashions—personified by the "geek-chic" of Elvis Costello and David Byrne—New Wave was the "anti-disco," even though several of its practitioners (notably Human League and Ultravox) shamelessly plundered disco's dance rhythms.

PERFORMING ON "THE MIDNIGHT SPECIAL"

PLEASE DON'T GO

BY H.W. CASEY AND R. FINCH
USED BY PERMISSION FROM EMI LONGTITUDE PUBLISHING AND HARRICK MUSIC

I love you
Yeah
Babe, I love you so
I want you to know
That I'm going to miss your love
The minute you walk out that door
[Chorus]

So please don't go
Don't go
Don't go away
Please don't go
Don't go
I'm begging you to stay
If you leave
At least in my lifetime
I've had one dream come true
I was blessed to be loved
By someone as wonderful as you
[Chorus]

Hey, hey, hey
Yeah
Babe, I love you so
I, I want you to know
That I'm going to miss your love
The minute you walk out that door
So please don't go
Don't go
Don't go away
Hey, hey, hey
I need your love
I'm down on my knees
Beggin' please, please, please
Don't go
Don't you hear me baby

Please don't go

Don't leave me now
Oh, no, no, no, no
Please don't go
I want you to know
That I, I, I, love you so
Don't leave me baby
Please don't go

On January 15, 1982, KC, already buffeted by the changing musical winds, was forced to deal with an entirely different sort of setback. While driving his car, he was seriously hurt in a head-on collision only a few blocks from home. The resulting concussion and pinched nerve required nine months of rehabilitation, and only seemed to emphasize his increasingly tenuous grip on things.

It made him realize, he says, "that you have no control over the destiny of your life, really. I think you file it away the same way as the (Rio) elevator experience," he says now. "It brings a lot of realization to your life about how human you really are. I think we forget how vulnerable we are to many different things."

He also discovered his vulnerability to addiction as he found himself increasingly dependent on the painkillers his doctors prescribed to aid his recuperation.

His hospitalization wasn't all bad news. KC met a young fan there, a 16-year-old girl who had also been seriously hurt in a traffic accident. "She was down the hall from me and she'd been hit by a car," he recalls. "They came by and said: 'Would you mind going down there and cheering her up a little bit?' So, it became a daily thing for me, to go down in my wheelchair to see her. I think she was getting out on Valentine's Day, so I gave her a little bear that had a heart on it."

Twenty years later, KC would receive an email from out of the blue. It was from the young girl, now a woman in her 30s, who wrote to say she still remembered his act of kindness. He smiles: "The email mentioned how she still had the teddy bear..."

Musically, there was little to smile about during this hexed period of his life. Case in point. In August of '83, **Give It Up**, a single from *All In A Night's Work*, had been released by Epic's Irish division, and had rocketed to the top of the charts in Britain.

It was fresh validation, a sign that KC's instincts for hit-writing hadn't died with the disco craze. Perversely, his American parent label refused to release the song as a single in the United States, even after the compelling evidence of its No. 1 status overseas. For KC, it was the frustrating culmination of a bad business decision—signing with Epic, which dropped him from its roster shortly afterwards.

"In a way, Epic was going to be a step up from T.K. because T.K. was the kind of company that didn't do that much marketing," he says with a rueful grin.

KC CIRCA 1980 ●●●●

With Epic refusing to release **Give It Up** as a single, KC took matters into his own hands. He formed his own company and distributed the song at the end of '83. Instant vindication. Even without the clout of a major label behind it, the song went to No. 18 on the charts, and its national airplay reflected even wider popularity.

But KC would fall deeper into despondency a few months later when his father, Harry, died in March of 1984.

"I think he was just one of the greatest men on Earth," says his only son. "He was strict in his ways. He didn't hesitate to take the belt off, and if the belt came off it got used. It didn't just come off for show."

His father, who had run a Miami furniture store when KC was young and later worked as a postman, was famous for his aphorisms. A fool and his money are soon parted. Never expect life to serve you your portion on a silver platter.

KC adds, "He knew how important common sense is in life. He was not always one to say I love you. It was just understood."

With his father gone, his major label deal kaput, and an increasing drug dependency, KC made the decision, in 1985, to step away from public life. The 34-year-old star, who had savored the spotlight and courted attention for more than a decade, became a furtive homebody, a recluse living behind the gates of his Miami Lakes hideaway.

They say that the human personality is informed by conflicting impulses, opposite tendencies which merge to create new versions of selfhood. So it is that an essentially shy person can become an apparent extrovert, craving attention even as his inner self recoils from the applause.

Fermin Goytisolo, who has performed with KC in front of millions of people for more than a quarter century now, believes his old friend is a laid back soul, essentially an introvert who willed himself into becoming one of the great performers of his generation.

"When you put the camera on him at the beginning, like when we did (the '70s music show) *Don Kirshner's Rock Concert*, you could see it," says Goytisolo. "You could call it shyness. He's down to earth. And he always stayed that way. He went through a lot and came back."

Says KC of his self-imposed exile: "I really didn't want to be told what to do any more, where to be, when to smile, when to laugh. I wanted to wake up when I wanted to wake up, wanted to go to bed when I wanted to go to bed. I didn't want to have any restrictions.

"Things were just so hectic," he says with a shrug. "I was with these managers and all these people, it was just too much. I didn't know how else to do it but to bring everything down to zero, even if that meant losing everything, giving up everything."

While most performers take scheduled breaks from their careers, this was different, this was an escape. "I thought of it as permanent." he says. "I've never had a middle—it's either all the way or no way at all with me. That's not good. I wish I had a 'middle' sometimes.

"What I guess I really did at 'zero' was getting into the drugs and partying and that kind of thing. But even though I was doing the wrong things I was still happy, to a point."

He manages a grim laugh, "Then all of a sudden you're praying, 'Oh, God, get me off of this. I'm gonna die.' Then there was just this wake up call."

IT'S EITHER ALL THE WAY OR NO WAY AT ALL WITH ME. THAT'S NOT GOOD.

I WISH I HAD A 'MIDDLE' SOMETIMES

GIVE IT UP

BY H. W. CASEY AND D. CARTER
USED BY PERMISSION FROM HARRICK MUSIC

Everybody wants you
Everybody wants your love
I'd just like to make you mine, oh mine

Nana nana nana nana na na now
Baby give it up, give it up, baby give it up
Nana nana nana nana na na now
Baby give it up, give it up, baby give it up

Everybody sees you
Everybody looks and stare
I'd just like to make you mine, oh mine

Nana nana nana nana na na now
Baby give it up, give it up, baby give it up
Nana nana nana nana na na now
Baby give it up, give it up, baby give it up

Give it up

Nana nana nana nana na na now
Baby give it up, give it up, baby give it up
Nana nana nana nana na na now
Baby give it up, give it up, baby give it up

Everybody wants you
Everybody wants your love
I'd just like to make you mine, oh mine

Nana nana nana nana na na now
Baby give it up, give it up, baby give it up
Nana nana nana nana na na now
Baby give it up, give it up, baby give it up

When you give it, can you give it, give it up
Come on baby I need your love
Give it up some I can love
Come on and play the game of love
Everybody is at need, give it up
Come on baby I need your love
Can I touch you, can I love you
Come on baby, baby I love you
Can you give it, give it up

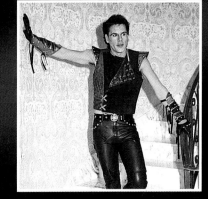

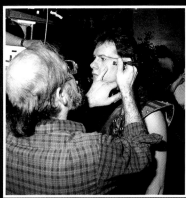

GIVE IT UP VIDEO SHOOT

Mel Haber – "Uncle Mel" to his friends – does not look like anybody's guardian angel. In fact, Haber more closely resembles an old borscht belt comic with his smiling features and melodic speaking cadence, which evokes the rhythms of a bygone era.

Haber, a financial advisor by trade, has been KC's Florida-based business manager for the past 15 years. "KC is one of the greatest entertainers I have ever had the pleasure of knowing," says Haber.

Mel, an old showbiz hand who once hosted his own radio show in south Florida and knows his way around celebrities from his days as a theatre owner, was KC's best last chance to dig himself out of the hole into which he'd fallen.

"I found Mel and he helped me reorganize my life," says KC. "I had had all these people around me who were 'yessing' me all the time. I was just with these bad people – things were going from bad to worse."

Acting on KC's behalf, Haber enlisted the services of KC's old friend and backing singer, Beverly Foster, who knew the music business better than Haber. Together, they began booking new shows.

It was tough sledding at first, as KC, still doing drugs and living the life of a semi-recluse, struggled to meet his new commitments.

"He always delivered, though," says Foster. "He always showed up, even when you could tell it was difficult for him."

With fresh bookings and a renewed public interest in the music of the '70s, the '90s seemed to lay ahead for KC like a shining road to redemption. There was just one catch. He was still using drugs. No comeback could be complete until he found a way to kick the habit.

TOP TO BOTTOM

Mel Haber

Beverly Foster

I FELT CLEAN, I FELT FRESH,

I FELT 21 AGAIN.

By 1995, KC was ready to finally confront his addiction, and checked himself into a treatment center in Durham, North Carolina.

"I just started feeling that if I'm going to do this I can't do it the way I've been doing it," he says of his decision to get clean.

He says he originally planned "to go into lock-up," where detox patients are put under strict surveillance, but he scotched that plan.

"After you come out, you have to live a life," he reasoned. "I figured being in a lock-up is not being part of life. It's not reality."

In North Carolina, he was a day patient, staying across the street from the facility each night and going in each day for meals and therapy.

For each 24-hour period off drugs, he attached a twinkly, stick-on star to the back of his clinic i.d. pass. "I felt clean, I felt fresh, I felt 21 again. It was like I had my life back."

IT WAS LIKE I HAD MY LIFE BACK

SHINE
THE RETURN OF A LEGEND

• • • • •

WHEN I WANTED TO CHANGE, NO ONE WOULD ALLOW ME TO CHANGE.

THEY ALWAYS WANTED IT

Every great musician, and certainly a few who aren't so great, eventually end up being pigeon-holed by their public, imprisoned by the identities they established for themselves during their first great brush with fame.

From The Beach Boys to The Rolling Stones, the demand to roll out the old hits is ceaseless, and can cause less resilient artists to creatively wither in the face of their fans' all-consuming nostaglia. It's why The Beach Boys still do nightly versions of *Little Deuce Coupe* and *Good Vibrations*, four decades after they were first written and performed, and why The Stones continue to treat *Sympathy For The Devil* as a major set-piece in their live shows.

Much as he still enjoys playing his old songs, KC, too, has felt the asphyxiating tug of nostalgia: "I've always felt like I've never been allowed to grow," he says. "When I wanted to change, no one would allow me to change. They always wanted it to be like **Get Down Tonight**."

Actually, it was a double bind. When he would try to deliver new songs in the old style he was rebuffed for doing that, too. "They'd say, 'Well, it sounds dated.' I'm going: 'What the hell do you want? This is what you said you wanted!'"

But for KC, a funny thing happened on the way to that Great Cosmic Delete Bin, where older artists are expected to go when the world no longer cares about their new ideas. He bumped into "Lou."

TO BE LIKE GET DOWN TONIGHT

"We're bringing KC and The Sunshine Band into the new millenium," says Lou Pearlman, who knows a thing or two about arranging chart supremacy for his recording acts.

Pearlman is the Orlando-based impresario who groomed two of the late-20th century's global monsters – The Backstreet Boys and 'N Sync, a one-two marketing punch that redefined contemporary pop music through its intensive work ethic, close vocal harmonies and sleek, hypercaffeineted choreography.

While Pearlman's boy-bands might seem far removed from the old-school stylings of KC, Pearlman saw in KC's songs the very foundations of what he had conjured with The Boys and 'N Sync. In fact, it's hard to imagine bands like 'N Sync existing without the pioneering influence of KC, who brought insistent dance beats, kinetic stage moves and certifiably infectious pop music to the American public 25 years earlier.

"KC is a legend," says Pearlman. "Everybody knows his music. You'll see it in commercials, you'll hear it everywhere. The bottom line is it's time for him to rekindle the flame."

TOP TO BOTTOM

Lou Pearlman with KC
at his 50th birthday party

KC signing with Lou Pearlman
of Trans Continental Records

"Rekindling the flame is what we do best," adds Pearlman, who has recently gone into the studio with KC to record new music for what they hope will be a breakthrough album. "We want to modify it from the '70s sound and bring it up to current dance sounds," says Pearlman. "The difference between disco and dance is not much."

Says KC: "Lou's a great guy. He came to one of my shows at the House Of Blues a couple of years ago and asked me what I was doing, and that's how we started working together. I think he just sees that my type of sound is missing out there a little bit—that raw sound of the '70s—and I think he feels we can recapture some of that, if not all of it."

Says longtime Florida deejay Footy, a morning-show fixture at Miami's Y-100 and a longtime supporter of KC's music: "When he gets in there with Lou, I expect to see a number of hits come out of it. KC's understanding of the beat is timeless —it doesn't really change."

"Lou is a very brilliant man," says KC. "A brilliant marketer. He has his finger on the pulse of what's going on."

Pearlman also happens to be a former musician. "It's not that well known about me but I played the New York club circuit through the disco era," says Pearlman, who is first cousin to singing legend Art Garfunkel of Simon and Garfunkel fame.

"My group Flyer opened up for Kool & The Gang, Donna Summer, Gloria Gaynor, Barry White, and, not only that, we opened for KC and The Sunshine Band! This was way before we knew each other," adds the guitarist turned entrepreneur. "He'd hardly remember, because we were just a small little pea-in-a-pod that never made it big. But KC made it big. And he's going to be very big again."

Billy Sammeth, KC's longtime personal manager, sees the Pearlman/KC pairing as a natural fit.

"Lou is bigger than life," says Sammeth, adding that he recently caught Pearlman on a TV talk show, where he described KC and The Sunshine Band as "my other boy band."

Laughs Sammeth: "That's just Lou's passion about having a hit with KC again. I'm expecting great things from that relationship."

HE'S A MENSCH. YOU ALWAYS SEE HIM
OUT AND AROUND FOR GOOD CAUSES

AMERICAN SOAP BOX DERBY, AKRON, OHIO, 1980 ●●●●●●

If you don't live in south Florida, it might be hard to grasp the importance of Harry Wayne Casey, not only on the local music scene, where he gave birth to the Miami Sound and helped put the region on the map, but in the way he has always been there for his community.

"He's a mensch," says one local admirer. "You always see him out and around for good causes."

Footy, who's been a radio kingpin in south Florida for the past 28 years, says that KC's dedication to charity is tireless. Y-100's annual Wing Ding, a two-day music festival which features top stars performing in aid of Here's Help (a residential and outpatient program for adolescents and young adults trying to kick drugs), is in many ways a KC-driven affair.

"KC has been a fantastic supporter of our efforts at the Wing Ding," Footy says of the event, which draws more than 75,000 fans through its gates and is now in its 16th year. "KC has performed probably 10 times. Not only does he donate his performance but it costs him a lot of money to do it. He foregoes his well-deserved fee and also incurs expenses of his own."

KC also makes regular visits to Here's Help's various city-wide outreach programs. Footy recalls the time KC strolled through the charity center's commons, an outdoor space where kids go to grab a breath of fresh air between classes.

"In the afternoon the sun hits right on that area," says Footy. "Turns it into an anvil, it's so hot. KC stops and says: 'Hey, this is murder out here. We've got to do something about it.' So we ordered an awning to shade the area, which cost over $7,000, and KC wrote a cheque to pay for the whole thing.

"To us, he's really a God and an inspiration. His performances at the Wing Ding have raised probably hundreds of thousands of dollars."

As someone whose own career dates back to the early '70s, Footy is in a unique position to appreciate how his friend's celebrity informs the spirit of modern Miami.

"There are three superstars that live in south Florida—Gloria Estefan, Dan Marino (former Miami Dolphins quarterback) and KC," says Footy. "If you like, you could add to that list The Bee Gees and Lenny Kravitz."

"But KC, I call him one of The Big Three. He is the heartbeat of Miami. KC, musically, put Miami on the map, and I think culturally and in terms of hipness. KC definitely made Miami hip. We were a redneck hicktown before that."

LEFT: KC AT THE Y-100 CONCERT IN BICENTENIAL PARK, DOWNTOWN MIAMI, 1976
RIGHT: KC FOR MUSCULAR DYSTROPHY, 1979

Most folks from the region will confirm the love that Floridians feel for KC, but Miami entertainment lawyer David Bercuson, who has represented the singer for several years, offers a story to illustrate the point.

KC WITH SISTER SAVINA

A couple of years ago, he and KC's Florida business manager Mel Haber went out for dinner with KC to a local steakhouse, where KC was on friendly terms with most of the staff.

"While we were in the middle of dinner, an older waiter a couple of tables away just grabbed his chest and fell down and passed out on the floor," Bercuson recalls. "Ultimately, he passed away in the hospital.

"The reaction in the restaurant was very strange. There were a lot of people that just got up and ran off and left their checks. But the thing that was so amazing was that every single waitress went to KC to get a hug and a kiss. He was so warm and so gentle and so caring for all the people in the restaurant. They all went to him—they didn't go to their manager or the maitre d'. They all gravitated to KC.

"He even went to the hospital with some of the waitresses to take care of them and to take care of the man's family," Bercuson continues. "It was so meaningful to me, because my (law) practice is all music and television. I've seen a lot of artists, and some are wonderful people, but this was just so out of the ordinary. People just feel so comfortable around him that they need to be with him in difficult moments."

LEFT TO RIGHT: CASEY, MONTGOMERY, SHAWN AND CHANEL, KC'S NIECES AND NEPHEWS

KC's current bandmates also tell stories about their leader's extraordinary kindness.

"Two years ago we had a show in Texas," says Zeljko Marinovic, who's played keyboards in The Sunshine Band for the past five years. "The stage was made of wood, and in one part of the stage there was a hole, so KC during the show accidentally stepped into the hole and fell down and ruptured a disc in his back.

"So he had an operation and we didn't play for three months. And it was questionable if he was ever going to walk again. Thank God after three months he recovered and everything was OK. But even for that three months that we didn't play, he sent us cheques so that we could survive.

"That was really cool of him. He didn't have to do that."

When told of Marinovic's comments, KC shrugs. "Of course they got paid—they're my band."

Harry Wayne Casey has always understood the disconnect between the booty-shaking icon who revolutionized dance music in the '70s and the person he is right at this moment, nuzzling his dogs in the lengthening shadows of a sunny Florida afternoon on his screened-in deck.

"When I was growing up I had a nickname, 'Sparky', which my whole family called me all my life, never called me any part of my real name," he smiles.

"But when I went to school they called me Harry and when I went to work I started using the last name of Casey (ergo, KC). So if someone called me Harry I knew I went to school with them and if someone called me Casey I knew I must have worked with them and if they called me Sparky then I knew they must have been a relative or a neighborhood kid."

Perhaps his greatest talent, apart from music, is the way he has let all of those names, and what each implies about him, play a role in his life.

Disc jockeys and steakhouse waitresses might be in awe of someone who comports himself as a star, but they can only love a person willing to step out of his carefully-controlled persona. Says KC: "I remember when it started happening for me (in the mid '70s), it was important for me to keep saying in my mind: 'Stay who you are. Stay who you are.'"

TOP TO BOTTOM

○ Henry Stone, KC
and Steve Alaimo
○ Mark Powers, Savina and KC
○ Michael Tramp, KC
and Fleur his designer

Billy Sammeth's relationship with KC dates back to the late '70s, when Sammeth, the now-legendary West Coast talent manager, was working for Katz-Gallin, the Los Angeles agency KC was then signed to.

At Katz-Gallin, Sammeth was KC's personal manager, so the two have been through basically everything together.

"He's still a little kid," says Sammeth, 50, who resumed his professional relationship with KC in the mid-'90s. "The reason we get along so well? We're all like little kids on the tour bus. We're pretty well happy all the time.

"KC's always happy. He really is. He loves performing. He loves meeting his fans. He loves being on stage. He has a real passion, still."

It wasn't always so, Sammeth admits.

KC'S MOM'S FAMILY

HE'S THE MOST NORMAL PERSON I KNOW.
HE STILL LIVES IN THE SAME HOUS

"He lost his passion during that dark period when he needed to go into rehabilitation. He lost that happiness, I know that. I could tell when I was getting phone calls from him in the middle of the night—and he was just waking up! Listen, it was a very courageous move on his part to get the help. It saved his life.

"We used to talk about it on the phone," Sammeth says. He remembers saying to KC, "As a friend who adores you, you need to do this to save your life."

HE LIVED IN 30 YEARS AGO

Sammeth believes that through all the tribulation and pain, through the isolating extremes and nerve-fraying distractions of being a pop superstar, KC has never really forgotten his mantra of "Stay who you are."

"You know how a lot of times celebrities are sort of isolated from their public?" says Sammeth. "He never is. He's never isolated from his group."

Sammeth laughs: "He's the most normal person I know. He still lives in the same house he lived in 30 years ago. It's a real comfort zone for him. He loves that house, even though he says he's going to move..."

Sammeth lets the sentence trail off, leaving the impression that KC is staying put.

Even without the events of 2002—including his star on Hollywood's Walk Of Fame—the comeback of Harry Wayne Casey has been remarkable.

"He's busier now than when he was a kid," says David Bercuson. "Everybody knows about the great success of licensing his music for compilation records and movies, literally around the world. And also the use of his music in advertising all over television and radio."

A partial list of KC's ad credits confirms his fresh cachet in the marketplace. Recent or current commercial clients include Old Navy (**Give It Up/Keep It Comin' Love**), Toyota (**That's The Way (I Like It)**), Amoco (**Please Don't Go**), Budweiser (**Get Down Tonight**), Denny's (**Keep It Comin' Love**), Old El Paso/Pillsbury (**I'm Your Boogie Man**) and Kraft Shake & Bake (what else? **Shake Your Booty**).

"Some writers do not want their music used that way," KC mused in a 1998 interview with Jim Sullivan in *The Boston Globe*. "I don't think it hurt. The songs are commercial, and why not tie them in with a commercial?"

As proof of the enduring popularity of KC's classic song catalogue, *The Best Of KC and The Sunshine Band,* a greatest hits compilation released on Rhino Records, went gold in 1999, pushing the group's lifetime, worldwide sales past the 100 million mark.

The concert trail has also yielded strong notices. One critic, reviewing a Connecticut show in July 2001, called the songs "insanely catchy." Another rhapsodized about the "outrageous stage show"—a welter of rainbow-hued lighting effects, dry ice, and "a large silver ball hanging above the stage that reflected colored lights throughout the theatre, making it reminiscent of a disco nightclub of the mid-'70s."

Despite its obvious homage to the past, Footy points out that there is nothing conceptually dated about KC's current show. "You can't speak of KC in the past tense. He's very contemporary. He's still a great performer and he makes great new music."

LEFT TO RIGHT: KC WITH BRITNEY SPEARS ON THE SET OF "LONGSHOT", KC WITH HANSON, KC ON THE SET OF AUSTIN POWERS 3 WITH BEYONCE KNOWLES OF DESTINY'S CHILD

At Miami's Wing Ding festival, sharing the bill with youth acts like Britney Spears and Hanson, "the younger artists all ran out in the crowd to see him," reports Footy. Destiny's Child were apparently so keen to watch KC perform "they snuck out into the audience with baseball hats on to disguise themselves."

Adds Sammeth, warming to an anecdote: "The mark of a great artist is how their music stands the test of time." He remembers when Bill Clinton was leaving the White House, and how a fan of the outgoing president held up a now-famous sign (quoting the Sunshine Band song) **Please Don't Go**.

"All these cultural references started with KC," muses Sammeth. "**That's The Way (I Like It)**—whenever there's a great play at a football game, that's what they play over the PA system. And I don't think I've ever gone to a baseball game when they haven't played **Shake Your Booty**. Ever!"

What's most encouraging in these early days of the new millennium, as America tries to put the terrible events of September 11 behind it, is that the spirit of KC's music has never seemed fresher or more purposeful.

"I really feel there's a sound missing out there," he smiles as he basks in the last slanting rays of a quiet day. "It's kind of a cross between funk and rock with horns.

"Hey, I'm reaching my 30-year cycle," he laughs. "It's definitely time again."

I'LL BE THERE FOR YOU

WRITTEN BY H. W. CASEY AND D. CABRERA
USED BY PERMISSION FROM HARRICK MUSIC AND CABABRA PRODUCTIONS

Telling you no secrets baby telling you no lies
Everything about you bringing tears to my eyes
Tell you baby if you only knew uh
That I'll be there for you
Standing right through all the struggle and the strife
Every single minute through the haze and the daze of our lives
If you only knew uh
I'll be right there for you

[Chorus]

Oh if you want me too I'll be there for you
I'll be there for you yeah yes
Oh if you want me too I'll be there for you
I want too I want too
I want to be there for you

Sometimes you feel that you're down so low
You don't know which way you're even gonna go
All you need to know is that uh
I'll be there for you
If you start to think you can't make another day
Life just seems to be getting in your way
All you need to know is that uh
I'll be there for you

[Chorus]

No matter how dark no mater how dim
You always seem to lose and never seem to win
If you only knew uh
I'll be there for you
Anytime anywhere anything you need
All you have to do is reach out for me
Uh if you only knew
I'll be there for you

[Repeat 1st verse]

Yes I will
Oh, hmmmmmmmm
Right there right there
Yeah yeah, ow, yeah yeah
Ow, right there, right there for you
Yeah yeah yeah
Mmm I'll be there yes I will yes I will

GOLD SINGLES

QUEEN OF CLUBS
[England]

GET DOWN TONIGHT
[United States, England, Holland, Canada, Japan]

THAT'S THE WAY [I LIKE IT]
[United States, England, Holland, Canada, Japan]

[SHAKE, SHAKE, SHAKE] SHAKE YOUR BOOTY
[United States, Japan]

I'M YOUR BOOGIE MAN
[United States, Canada]

KEEP IT COMIN' LOVE
[United States, Canada]

PLATINUM SINGLES

I'M YOUR BOOGIE MAN

GOLD ALBUMS

KC AND THE SUNSHINE BAND
[United States, Canada, Australia]

PART 3
[United States, Canada]

THE BEST OF KC AND THE SUNSHINE BAND
[United States]

PLATINUM ALBUMS

KC AND THE SUNSHINE BAND
[United States, Canada]

PART 3
[United States, Canada]

WHO DO YA LOVE
[United States]

DO YOU WANNA GO PARTY
[United States]

DOUBLE PLATINUM ALBUM

PART 3
[United States]

GRAMMY AWARDS

BEST RHYTHM & BLUES VOCAL
PERFORMANCE BY A GROUP 1975
[Get Down Tonight]

BEST NEW ARTIST 1975

BEST R&B SONG [writers award] 1975
[Get Down Tonight]

BEST R&B SONG [writers award] 1975
[That's The Way [I Like It]]

BEST R&B SONG [writers award] 1975
[Where Is The Love] WINNER

ALBUM PRODUCER OF THE YEAR 1978
[Saturday Night Fever] WINNER
Harry W. Casey

ALBUM OF THE YEAR 1978
[Saturday Night Fever] WINNER
KC and The Sunshine Band

AMERICAN MUSIC AWARDS

BEST NEW GROUP 1975 WINNER

BEST R&B VOCAL PERFORMANCE
BY A GROUP 1976 [Shake Your Booty]

BEST POP VOCAL PERFORMANCE
BY A GROUP 1977 [Keep It Comin' Love]

BEST R&B VOCAL PERFORMANCE
BY A GROUP 1977 [Keep It Comin' Love]

DISCO MUSIC AWARDS

BEST MIXED GROUP

JUNO AWARDS [CANADA]

BEST INTERNATIONAL GROUP
[Shake Your Booty]

ACKNOWLEDGMENTS

The author wishes to acknowledge the help and kindness of several people, without whom this project could not have moved forward with such grace and dispatch. My greatest debt is to KC himself, who warmly opened up his home for interviews over the busy Super Bowl Weekend, and who provided us with literally cartons of vintage photographs and personal effects, many of which appear in the pages of this book.

The author also wishes to thank our "Florida Response Team"—the indefatigable and multi-talented Irene Marie, who conducted interviews with KC, excerpts of which appear in this book, and who offered unerring advice on the design and conceptual themes which you see before you.

Special thanks to Irene's right-hand lady, Allee Newhoff-Mendoza, who not only did interviews with members of KC's current band and shared her musical insights in countless editorial meetings, but worked the phones and helped nudge the book along in any number of ways with her tireless good cheer.

Endless gratitude to our design team in Montreal, the wonderful Julie Desilets, Geneviève Desrosiers and Nathalie Michaud, whose artistic direction enlivens these pages and helps tell the KC story with the verve and panache he so richly deserves.

In this endeavor, they were ably led by renowned south Florida photographer Marc Serota, who caught KC's performances right from the stage's edge, and who gamely traipsed from Miami to Las Vegas to Chicago in search of the perfect shot.

Thanks also to KC's management team, including manager Bill Sammeth and lawyer David Bercuson, who provided insight and advice in building the KC story arc, and who helped arrange interviews during the mad dash of February and March when researching and writing kicked into high gear.

Thanks, finally, to Allan "Turtle" Turowetz, whose vision and zeal brought this book to fruition, and whose sharp editorial eye aided immeasurably in conjuring the giddy ambience and boogie-till-you-drop spirit of disco-era America.

To everyone else, see you on the dance floor!

JOINTLY PUBLISHED BY
Team Power Publishing Inc.
Éditions du Trécarré Inc.
Irene Marie Publishing

AUTHOR
Craig MacInnis

EDITOR IN CHIEF
Allan Turowetz

DIRECTOR OF PHOTOGRAPHY
Marc Serota

VISUAL CONSULTANT
Irene Marie

CREATIVE DIRECTOR
Julie Desilets

ART DIRECTOR
Nathalie Michaud

GRAPHIC DESIGN | COMPUTER GRAPHICS
Nathalie Michaud, Brigitte Boudrias

CO-ORDINATOR | RESEARCHER
Geneviève Desrosiers, Allee Newhoff-Mendoza

PICTURES BY:
Courtesy of Harry Wayne Casey and family
pgs. 16, 20-21, 24, 32 thru 103 (38 thru 55 by Larry G. Warmoth), 108, 112-113, 115, 116, 118, 119, 123

Marc Serota
pgs. 4, 8-9, 10, 12-13 (courtesy of Florida Marlins) 14-15, 22-23, 25, 26, 28-29, 30-31, 104 thru 107, 110, 114

Navid
Stylist Samantha Weston
pgs. 2-3, 18-19, 109, 117, 120-121

David Vance, *pgs. 6 & 125*

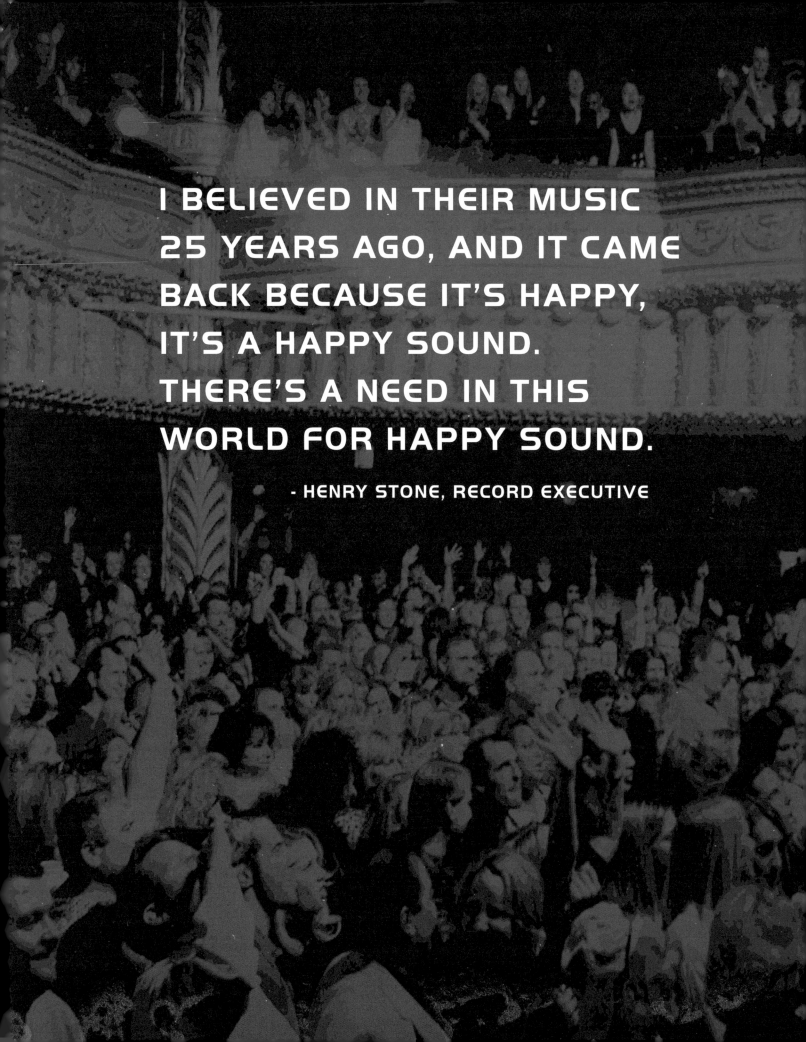

I BELIEVED IN THEIR MUSIC
25 YEARS AGO, AND IT CAME
BACK BECAUSE IT'S HAPPY,
IT'S A HAPPY SOUND.
THERE'S A NEED IN THIS
WORLD FOR HAPPY SOUND.

- HENRY STONE, RECORD EXECUTIVE